Divergent Paths

Divergent Paths

NAVIGATING SEPARATION WITH LOVE AND RESPECT

DR. SILMA QUIÑONES

PRIMIX
PUBLISHING
THE WRITE CHOICE

Primix Publishing
485c US Highway 1 South
Suite 100
Iselin, NJ 08830
www.primixpublishing.com
Phone: 1-800-538-5788

Published by Primix Publishing: 09/11/2024

ISBN: 979-8-89194-332-2(sc)
ISBN: 979-8-89194-333-9(e)

Contents

Introduction vii

When Love Fades Away: Identifying the First Signs 1

Navigating Mixed Feelings When Deciding to Separate 23

The Fear of a Partner's Violent Reaction 35

Caught Between a Rock and a Hard Place: Facing the

    Threat of Suicide. 42

The Reaction of Family and Friends. 45

Communicating the Decision: Approaching the Topic of

    Separation with Empathy and Understanding. 50

Freeing Yourself from the Burden: Guilt Feelings in

    Separation 57

The Fear of Loneliness after Separation. 62

The Separation and its Impact on Children 67

The Separation Process: Steps and Considerations. 71

Handling the Perception of Abandonment. 76

Final Reflections 81

Introduction

As a psychologist, much of my work involves assisting individuals who are contemplating leaving their partners. On numerous occasions, the response to my initial question, "What motivates you to seek help?" has been as follows: *"Doctor, I'm not sure if I'm wrong, but I don't want to make mistakes. I've been reflecting for a while now, and I feel like the love has disappeared in my relationship. I no longer have sexual desires, and instead of spending time with him, I prefer to be with other people. Even when I think about going back home, I find excuses to delay. I go to the supermarket, to the stores, or run any errands before coming home. However, the idea of separating terrifies me; I'm afraid of regretting it. I wonder if this is just a passing phase or if the problem is me. I dare not speak about this out loud, not even with my friends or family. Sometimes, I think about the pain it would cause them, and for now, I prefer to cling to the hope that something magical can revive our love and save the relationship."*

I've met people who are distressed because their partners have expressed the desire to end their relationship. For instance, one person shared: *"I'm suffering a lot because my partner told me he no longer wants to continue the relationship with me. I spend my time crying, and I can't sleep. I get desperate when I call him, and he doesn't answer the phone. I can't imagine my life without him. I know we have our issues, and he suggested that we seek help, but I believe every relationship has its challenges. I'm willing to work on our problems, but he thinks it's too late. He advises me to seek help for myself because he doesn't love me anymore. Despite his denial, I feel that there is still love between us. I love him, and I don't want to give up."*

It is understandable that receiving that news is painful and triggers a series of emotions such as sadness, anger, uncertainty, shock, and fear of change. These emotions can be overwhelming, especially when they are provoked by contemplating the end of a relationship. This process is complex and painful, as emotions can arise unexpectedly. For example, you could be driving and suddenly feel the need to cry uncontrollably, or you could be at work experiencing anger and indignation at what your partner has said. The intensity of these emotions can make it difficult to remain calm or carry out daily tasks. Belief in the power of love and the idea that a lasting relationship is possible can lead to confusion when considering ending the relationship or facing a separation.

We often find it hard to accept the reality that divorce and separation rates are high. For instance, in Spain, the average length of marriages is about 16 years, and an estimated 12 marriages end in divorce every hour. Interestingly, only about 5% of divorced couples regret their decision and attempt to reconcile. On the other hand, couples who cohabit without being legally married tend to stay together for a shorter period than married couples. Separation is a challenging and painful process, and ending a romantic relationship can be more complicated than starting one.

The breakup of a romantic relationship ranks high on the list of factors that can trigger an emotional crisis. Separating from a partner generates more distress and tension than being incarcerated or losing a job. Both the person who decides to separate and the one who is left behind experience an emotional storm. Feelings like anger, sadness, frustration, anxiety, and desperation are common during this process, and they can lead to depression, neglect, and even suicide. The pain associated with a "broken heart" is real and can manifest, for example, as an intense pain in the chest that makes it difficult to maintain daily routines. In the brain, the region called the insula is activated in both physical pain situations and emotional breakups. Although the heart does not suffer an actual physical injury, the brain interprets it as a genuine wound.

Dealing with a breakup or coming to terms with the fact that we are no longer loved is an emotional challenge that is not easily overcome. It is important to understand that finding a new love doesn't automatically heal the pain of the breakup. Approaching the separation with seriousness, understanding, and understanding for each person involved, whether they are the one who leaves or the one who is left behind, is crucial. Romantic relationships are complex, and at times, parting ways may be a necessary decision for the well-being of both individuals. Let me offer you some reflection in this topic:

- Love is a powerful feeling and often makes us think about a shared future with a loved one. While we may hope for a lifetime together, the duration of a relationship does not determine its quality or success. It is essential to remember that effective communication, mutual trust, and compatibility are key elements for a healthy relationship, regardless of how long it lasts.

- Sometimes, the intense emotions of the first months or years can be confused with deep and eternal love, but it is important to understand that relationships evolve over time and can change. It is crucial to know that love requires effort, communication, and adaptation as circumstances and people evolve.

- The decision to stay with someone should not be based solely on momentary emotions. Healthy relationships also require compatibility, respect, and effective communication. It is important to recognize that there are toxic and unhealthy relationships where love is still present. In these cases, separation is most advisable, even if love for the person still exists.

• Relationships that do not last a lifetime are not necessarily a waste of time. During the relationship, there can be a lot of growth and changes in the way of seeing life and behaving. You may have matured and grown at a different pace than your partner, or vice versa. When this happens, the relationship can become complicated, not because it is toxic, but because it is no longer congruent with who you have become. Therefore, sometimes, separations can be opportunities for growth and learning.

• It is important to recognize when a relationship is no longer healthy and make decisions that benefit both parties. Recognizing the signs of a toxic or unhealthy relationship is fundamental for the emotional and mental well-being of both people involved. Making decisions that promote health and personal growth is essential to maintain positive and constructive relationships.

• The separation should not be considered a betrayal of religion or family. Every person deserves their happiness and well-being, and it is important to prioritize emotional well-being and authenticity in relationships. What seems to be an abandonment of religious values may be the reaffirmation of a deeper value, such as: "love your neighbor as you love yourself". You should not abandon self-love. Especially in romantic relationships, sacrificing your emotional and physical well-being for a relationship that is no longer healthy is not an affirmation of the values of most religions.

• Accepting that a relationship has ended can be painful, but it can also be liberating and allow us to move on to new experiences. The experience is an opportunity to reflect and make fundamental changes in our way of thinking, seeing life, acting, and behaving. Separating from an unhealthy relationship is an opportunity to reaffirm that we all can grow and be happy.

Ultimately, each relationship is unique, and the most important thing is that decisions are made with respect and care for oneself and the other. Separation is not always a failure. Sometimes, it is simply a new beginning. If you find yourself in a separation process, wether you initiated it or it was imposed on you, it is normal to feel like you are going through a crisis. The process and impact of separation depend on a multitude of complex factors, which carry a lot of emotional weight. Understanding those factors and how they will affect you will help you survive the crisis and grow with it. Although it may seem impossible, you can turn the separation process into an experience of significant personal growth. I have met women and men who live through the process with much suffering and despair. So much so that they contemplate suicide and physically deteriorate greatly. But after reflecting and changing their way of thinking and acting, they change how they feel. They grow in many ways, and after a while, most look younger, more attractive, and healthier.

I share Sara's example. After 22 years in a romantic relationship in which they had 3 children and a newborn grandchild, she decided to explore the possibility of separating from her husband.

She shares, "I kept myself in my role as a wife, faithful to what my parents and the church advised and expected of me. I got married very young, and within a year, I was already pregnant. Then I had two more children, one after the other. I dedicated myself to taking care of them and being a good homemaker. I have affection for my husband, but I don't feel love. His way of being bothers me a lot. From the beginning, we argued because he is very passive. He doesn't talk much, and I have to guess what he is thinking. Besides not telling me what he thinks and feels, he is very slow to make decisions, lacks initiative, and if it weren't for my insistence, we wouldn't even have a home. He doesn't cultivate friendships or take care of his family. He is happy going to work, coming home, having dinner, and sitting to watch TV until bedtime. We don't even have sex anymore. I am his servant. I wash his clothes, cook for him, clean the house, and take care of our children. I know that if I leave him, he will suffer because he will be t alone, and he does not know how to take care of himself."

Sara decided to get a divorce and initially, she appeared distraught during her counseling sessions. She seemed visibly worn out, prompting friends to question whether divorcing was the right choice. However, after a few months, I noticed a remarkable change in her. She appeared more vibrant, revamped her appearance and daily routine, became more socially active, and even secured a part-time job. She looked significantly younger. Recently, she mentioned that her friends envied her newfound peace, and some people even speculated that she had undergone plastic surgery due to her enhanced beauty.

As a psychologist, my goal is to help you navigate your emotions and find a healthy way to handle this challenge. Whether you are considering separation, have already made the decision to divorce, or have been informed that your partner no longer wants to continue in the relationship, the experience can have a profound impact on your life, whether positive or negative. My years of experience as a psychologist have allowed me to identify situations and challenges that are key to managing this situation so that you can learn and grow from this experience. This dialogue with you does not replace psychotherapy, but I share with you what I hope will help you understand more clearly what you are experiencing, make important decisions, and handle the experience with love, respect, and much personal growth.

When Love Fades Away: Identifying the First Signs

The announcement of the breakup of a relationship is not the beginning of a couple's separation. Generally, people reach the moment of official breakup after having experienced a long process of emotional separation. In my experience, I have observed that many people put off the decision to separate for too long due to fear of making mistakes and seeking to avoid the pain and setbacks that can arise from a breakup. "I don't want my children to suffer, I don't want my partner to suffer, nor my family who loves him so much." If the person feels some compassion, they tend to cling to that feeling to avoid causing what they understand will be a crisis for many.

One of my clients confessed to me that what made her seek

help was the death of her aunt's husband. She narrated, "We were at the funeral home, about to close the coffin, when the widow bursts into tears and demanded that they not take him away. I'm not ready, I can't, don't take him from me," my aunt shouted. I listened to her and remembered the saying, "After e three days, the dead stink". I thought, if he's dead, he's dead. At that moment, I identified with her resistance to accept the finality and understood that I was doing the same with my marriage. In order to avoid more suffering, I was denying the reality of the end of the relationship."

During our sessions following her sudden realization, she recognized her tendency to avoid challenging situations and decisions. She admitted that her hesitation to make decisions and follow through often caused her prolonged and unnecessary suffering. Upon finally taking action, she realized that delaying decisions did not make the outcome any less painful. She expressed deep regret and self-reproach for procrastinating for so long before taking action. " After years of hesitating, I deeply regret and blame myself for delaying the separation for so long."

Waiting for the *perfect time* to pursue independence after a separation can lead to missed opportunities for personal and financial growth. Procrastination may result in one's partner initiating the separation on terms that favor them, giving them the opportunity to control the narrative of the breakup and shift the blame onto the other person.

Some couples officially join even though they do not love each other, so in those cases, the separation begins even before the formal commitment. It is crucial to understand that mere cohabitation does not constitute a couple relationship if there is no genuine and voluntary commitment from both parties. In fact, countless factors can lead someone to break that commitment, as many as the reasons to love or stop loving. For example, many people who tolerate or forgive infidelity end up separating from their partners not because they were unfaithful but because they feel they are not receiving the attention they deserve. "I don't mind him occasionally seeking another woman to satisfy his manly needs, but it can't be that he gives her more gifts and attention than me. It hurts to find out that he enjoys artistic events with her, and he's not even willing to accompany me to a party with friends."

Others tolerate the lack of sexual passion but do not forgive their partner for lying to them. For example:

"I have already gotten used to only having sex with her from time to time. But it infuriates me that she hides the money she gives to her brother. She feels sorry for him, and when he asks her for money to pay his bills, she always helps him. Then she asks me for money because she doesn't have enough to pay her credit card bills, which makes me very angry. I know she doesn't tell me why she doesn't have enough money. She knows my opinion on the matter. Her brother is irresponsible, and she is willing to lie to me out of pity for him. She is betraying me when she lies to me. And I wonder if she also lies to me about other matters. I don't trust her anymore, and I increasingly doubt her sincerity. I don't even believe her when she tells me she loves me."

Some situations arise frequently in the couple's daily life that cause discomfort and displeasure. Some are simple but provoke intense and hurtful arguments. Here are some common complaints:

- Does not close the bathroom curtain.
- Does not put the toothpaste cap on, no matter how many times I ask her to do it.
- Does not put dirty clothes in the laundry basket.

- Does not pay bills on time.

- Does not turn off the lights when going to bed.

- Does not pay attention when I talk to her.

- Always on the phone.

- Does not dress or apply makeup on time to arrive on time to activities.

When two people come together in a romantic relationship, they bring with them behavior patterns, a variety of expectations, and multiple individual differences. At the beginning of the relationship, there is hope that despite these love and happiness and stability will prevail no matter what challenges life and the relationship bring. These challenges, although they may seem daunting, also present opportunities for growth and deeper understanding. However, in the process of interacting, especially if they live together as a couple, many conflicts, frictions, and difficulties arise. These can represent opportunities for growth, but they can also wear down the love they feel for each other.

These situations that seem trivial and without major consequences tend to produce a lot of resentment that accumulates until it causes the loss of love. They are habits that repeat on autopilot and frequently, in such a way that they provoke the interpretation that the partner does not change due to lack of interest on their part . and, worse still, due to lack of love. This perception is compounded by other instances that reaffirm to the couple that they are in a relationship with the wrong person. For the frustrated person, the relationship becomes an exercise in tolerance. They tolerate it because they are not ready to make the decision to break up the relationship over seemingly trivial matters. Some tolerate it for many years, while others do not. In reality, only each individual knows what their maximum tolerance level is. It cannot be predicted what will be the straw that breaks the camel's back. Recognizing the signs of intolerance and frustration is crucial for working on possible changes that can make for a healthier relationship.

In my office, I've heard both men and women recount the reasons that led them to consider separation. Often, it was not a sudden event, but a culmination of repeated behaviors that they had tolerated over the years. These behaviors, such as neglect, lack of communication, or disrespect, would cause frustration each time they occurred. Other examples of such behaviors could include lack of emotional support, constant criticism, or a failure to share responsibilities. With each instance, a discomfort that many describe as a *thorn in the heart* would arise. Once their tolerance was exhausted, there was no turning back despite a change in their behavior or improvements in other areas., The desire to stay in the relationship had faded, and they no longer felt love.

"Doctor, now he brings me coffee in bed, calls me during the day, and asks how I am, attentions that he never had with me and that now, instead of pleasing me, irritate me. Now it's too late. He should have done it when I asked."

If the partner is convinced that the failure of the relationship is due to the other person not making an effort, not understanding, or not being interested in changing, those challenges sow the seed of rupture. Separation begins when there is no willingness to make efforts to improve and conserve the relationship and not when difficulties or traumatic events arise. When one of the two people stops working to keep the relationship alive, that is when the separation begins.

Emotional abandonment and detachment from the relationship manifest in different ways. If you no longer feel love, it is very likely that the lack of love began when your partner did or said something that made you doubt their love. Initially, you might have felt loved, but a particular event or action caused you to doubt that love. For some people, this could be a betrayal, whether sexual or a lack of support during a critical time. For example, women place a high value on trust and support from their partner during difficult times. The absence of physical presence or attention during painful situations can make a woman feel alone and lead her to question the relationship.

A sign that the relationship will not last much longer is that the person is criticized a lot when problems or difficult situations arise. To criticize the partner instead of discussing the situation, either because it is believed that they caused the problem or because they don't seem to resolve it deteriorates the relationship. Common claims such as, "he/she doesn't understand me, doesn't listen to me, criticizes me so much that I don't feel loved" are indicative of this. When conversations turn into accusations and personal attacks, both parties can start to resent and disappoint each other.

The situation or incident that triggers the original

disappointment and complaint may be forgotten, but its negative impact lingers. Unconsciously, when a similar episode arises, the discomfort it produces adds to the previous ones. The passage of time does not diminish its importance or bring forgetfulness. Couples often recount incidents that occurred 10 years earlier with the same emotional intensity as they experienced in the original experience, underscoring the long-term impact of criticism.

Most of the time, a person abandons the commitment not because of a new and conflicting situation but because of an element that has always been present in the relationship. A couple comes to my office due to the frustration on the part of the man that his wife would humiliate him in front of the children. I share one, among many, of the examples that he recounted. "I stopped at a drive-thru to buy a hamburger because I was on my way home, tired, and very hungry. I called her to ask if she wanted me to buy something for her, as she really liked the hamburgers from the establishment. She tells me to bring her one with French fries. When I get home and hand her order, she complains that the sauce she always asks for with the fries is missing. She reproaches me: *Where is my favorite sauce? You know I always ask for that sauce. You always do the same thing! If I don't give you specific instructions, they don't occur to you. This was a simple task. You can be very smart for some things and so stupid and abnormal for others. You only think about yourself. I bet your order is complete. Of course, you first, second, third, and you don't care or think about the rest of us. Besides being stupid, you're selfish.* I stood in silence listening to her insults because I didn't want the kids to see us once again arguing in front of them."

The separation can come when the accumulation of that conflicting element reaches the person's maximum tolerance level. When the hope that the other person will change is lost, the lack of love deepens. In the relationship, the requested changes are accompanied by the conviction that the love for the person asking for the change will be motivation enough for them to make an effort and achieve the change. When the change does not occur, it is concluded that the failure is due to a lack of love. It is presumed that if the person does not change, it is because they are not interested in changing, and they are not interested in changing because there is no love. It is a logic that then leads to thinking, "Well, if they don't love me, I shouldn't love them."

This line of thought does not take into account that there are personality traits and behaviors that, no matter how much love or good intention there is, the person needs professional help to change. It's important to remember that seeking professional help is a valid and effective way to address relationship issues. On the other hand, sometimes, the person does not understand the request being made to them or does not recognize the urgency of the need to make the change and thinks they have time to change later. The fact is that the frustrated partner experiences their frustration as a lack of love. The separation can come when the accumulation of that conflicting element reaches the person's maximum tolerance level. The frustrated partner may no longer wish to remain in the relationship and no longer perceives their partner with the same love and affection.

On the other hand, some people experience a loss of love in just one instance or event. This loss of love is not tied to a series of events, repeated behaviors, or past memories. It's a powerful, immediate realization, as illustrated by the following example:

"When I first met her, I felt something special for her. But because of what she did yesterday, I realized that she doesn't love me. I feel that the special feeling I had for her suddenly died. In an instant, I no longer felt love for her."

Another person tells me, "In the last sexual encounter, he made a comment about my appearance. Then he insisted that it was just a mistake and that he wasn't thinking clearly when he said it. Since that incident, our intimacy has not been the same. Even the smell of him repulses me."

Likewise, separation can come from a particular experience related to a behavior that is considered intolerable, such as infidelity. Some of the people I have accompanied as a therapist have described this change in feeling in a very particular way. Let's see some examples:

Maria had been living with her partner for five years. Although they had faced many conflicts due to differences in working hours, economic difficulties, physical illnesses, and family situations, Maria felt committed to the relationship. One day, in the middle of a conversation, her partner revealed what she interpreted as his reluctance to accept and support her goal of having a professional career. "I don't know why you insist on studying so much to earn a minimum wage when I will always earn more money than you." His words deeply hurt her because she had always thought that he supported her as much as she supported him in his professional aspirations. Since then, Maria began to distance herself from her partner until they separated.

The revelation that her partner does not respect and support her talents and ambitions produced a feeling of betrayal and abandonment in her. These feelings contradict her expectations that a partner should be an ally and a partner in achieving goals and life ambitions.

While women today may fulfill some aspects of the traditional roles of a married woman, it is unacceptable that being in a relationship implies sacrificing her personal aspirations for the sake of their partner. This societal pressure, rooted in cultural beliefs, often leads to feelings of betrayal and abandonment, and is a common thread in the experience of infidelity.

Infidelity does not always arise for the same reasons or in the same way. Some people, out of immaturity, give themselves permission to enjoy a sexual encounter with another person trusting that they will not be discovered and that there will be no major consequences. Others have personality flaws that lead them to lie, avoid taking responsibility for their actions, act whimsically, and indulge in what they know is unacceptable. Additionally, some men believe that culturally, it is acceptable to be unfaithful as long as they fulfill their partner in other areas. Society and their culture give them permission to be unfaithful. At the extreme end of the infidelity spectrum are those who experience a significant sexual need and live with sexual addiction. For these individuals, even if sex in their relationship is positive, the frequency is not enough to satisfy their sexual needs and appetite. They may live in fear and anguish, dreading discovery and the resulting consequences, but they cannot control themselves.

Some immature individuals experience infidelity but later mature and realize that giving themselves permission was not correct and that losing their partner over sexual encounters is not worth it. If the infidelity is never verbalized and their partner never finds out, it can be mentally *archived* in the mind as a learning experience. It is not necessary to confess experiences or mistakes that are no longer repeated, and that the person has already overcome. This means that the individual acknowledges the mistake, learns from it, and moves on without the need to confess to their partner.

However, if the partner discovers and confronts them, the temptation to deny it is powerful. In my professional experience, accepting the facts and taking responsibility contributes much more to overcoming the crisis that arises when confronted with evidence of infidelity. When the person denies it to avoid consequences or to avoid causing emotional pain to their partner, it adds the element of lying and distrust bringing the situation to a much deeper and more difficult level to overcome. However, when the mistake is accepted, and responsibility for the actions is assumed, there is a resentment that is inevitable but can be healed. It takes time because it is a wound, and wounds do not heal overnight.

It is crucial to accept responsibility for unfaithful behavior. There should not be a half-hearted acceptance in which infidelity is justified, especially if it implies that the partner provoked the infidelity. Conflicts and grievances can be worked on in many other ways. Asking for forgiveness is a positive sign of repentance if it is sincere. However, there are people who tend to ask for forgiveness but as a form of manipulation and continue to make the same mistake.

If you suspect that your partner is still maintaining a relationship with another person, it is healthier to end the relationship and give them time to discover their true feelings. Witnessing your partner going out and coming back from romantic encounters with another person can be very painful, humiliating, and difficult to heal for self-esteem and personal pride. Ending the relationship allows you to heal and evaluate if the relationship is truly worth it and if you are willing to go through the necessary process to overcome such a deep wound.

On many occasions, I have observed how the person who ends the relationship manages to overcome the initial crisis while the unfaithful person continues with the other person for a while. Over time, they discover that the new partner does not offer what they valued in the previous relationship and return seeking a new opportunity. Some, on the other hand, seek out their ex-partner and turn them into their lover, reversing the roles. The one who was originally the spouse now becomes the lover.

If you are willing to forgive but fear making a mistake or fear not being able to heal the wounds, you can seek professional help to overcome the crisis. Forgiving does not require forgetting; forgiving means not punishing the person who has erred. For those who felt it was unfair to forgive without consequences, I suggested establishing a consequence or cost for the infidelity to set a limit. The cost or consequence could be a special gift, a whim for the partner who wants to forgive. This cost or consequence is determined by the person who has been cheated on, not the cheating person -just as the criminal does not determine the punishment. In my professional experience, when resentment or feelings of injustice arose, the granted gift eased the discomfort. Additionally, the cheating person was reminded that infidelity is not worth it every time they had to send the monthly gift payment, for example.

A sure sign that a lack of love is present in a relationship is the physical distance between both parties. The level of physical distance can reveal if they are attracted to each other. However, the distance between partners can also indicate how advanced and close their separation is. In the initial stages of a relationship, a pattern of wanting to be physically close is often observed. Lovers desire to see each other and share both public and private spaces. In social gatherings and with family members, it is common to see that where one is, the other is also. If one moves for some reason, shortly after, the other person follows to be close again. Where one goes, the other goes. If they are sitting on a couch, no matter how big it is, you see them very close together. When they walk down the streets, they hold hands or walk side by side. Common phrases that demonstrate the desire to be physically close include *Where should we meet?*, *Look for me*, and *I'll be there*. Although the relationship may become complicated and face challenges, if there is no loss of love, that pattern remains. I have seen couples who have been together for decades, and when they sit together, they do so with very little physical space between them.

On the other hand, I frequently observed a very particular pattern in couples experiencing a lack of love. When opportunities arise to be physically close or alone, instead of desiring and enjoying that intimate time without interruptions from children or acquaintances, they make plans to socialize with others. For example, they invite their friends for a barbecue in the backyard of their house. During the gathering, they focus on being hosts and "enjoying" the gathering. When it ends, they are so tired that they retire to their room to sleep and don't even share their impressions of the day.

Physical distance and a diminished sexual experience in a relationship often stems from unspoken resentments, kept secrets, lingering distrust, unaddressed disappointments, mistreatment, or neglect. It's not a result of the length of time a couple has been together or the presence of children Instead, it's a sign that there are issues that need to be openly discussed and resolved.

Another concerning behavior that contributes to emotional distancing is the attention given to cell phones at times when they could be conversing and enjoying each other's company. Often, couples can be seen in a restaurant, sitting across from each other but not talking or looking at each other. They are silently looking at their phones while waiting for the food. There is no dialogue about what they are reading or seeing on their phones. When served the food, they pay more attention to the waiter than to their partner.

Cruises and trips to tourist destinations are often seen as opportunities for couples to enjoy time together. The allure of taking a break from work and discovering new places and adventures is frequently promoted with images of happy, loving couples. Hotel rooms and picturesque pools contribute to the fantasy of experiencing intimate, magical, and unforgettable moments. However, if there is emotional distance in the relationship, when planning trips, they do so in groups, with friends or family. There are few moments when they are without distractions or interruptions from others. It seems like they are very sociable and enjoy spending time with family. However, the absence of physical intimacy is a sign that emotional intimacy is no longer the same as before. If that distance is not addressed in time, it can increase until it becomes insurmountable.

Anything that creates emotional distance and leads to a life not shared with your partner tends to contribute to separation. This does not mean that the relationship is in danger if one or both individuals can function independently. However, it is important to understand that being independent does not require excluding your partner from experiences. Work, children, friendships, religion, politics, and the family of origin can absorb a person to the point of excluding their partner. It is the individual who decides whether to allow themselves to be absorbed and abandon the relationship. Additionally establishing friendships, activities, and interests that you do not share with your partner increases the risk of contributing to the distance between you.

The process of emotional distancing and separation can also be influenced by situations we might not immediately recognize, such as differences in work schedules, that prevent the couple from spending time together. Let's see an example:

Pedro and Rosa had been married for six years. He worked a shift from 3 p.m. to 12 a.m., while she worked one from 8 a.m. to 5 p.m. When he returned from work, she was sleeping, and when she got up to go to work, he was sleeping. On Saturdays, she cleaned the house and went to the supermarket, while Pedro took care of the cars. On Sundays, they went to church together until noon, and in the afternoon, they visited their respective parents separately. Pedro and Rosa are a clear example of a couple that does not share a common life. Each one was creating a routine without including the other, and little by little, they were establishing friendships and interests that their partner did not share. When the idea of divorce arose in this case, both recognized that they had been emotionally separated for quite some time, even though they lived under the same roof.

If your relationship resembles that of Pedro and Rosa, and you are concerned about emotional distance, but you do not desire a separation, it is necessary to address what is causing the emotional and physical distance. If you have resentments, anger, or secrets, it is necessary that you work on eliminating them. Whether you seek professional help or undertake the task on your own, it is important that you do it as soon as possible. The longer time passes the more emotional distance increases. Once the process of falling out of love has started, it can only be stopped by the decision and commitment of both people to work together to save the relationship. Love is not recovered easily or spontaneously as when it originally arose.

As the couple fights and strives as a team to resolve those conflicts, even if they do not resolve them to their satisfaction, if they recognize that they made efforts together to face them, the relationship will grow and strengthen. This t is key to rescuing physical intimacy and reestablishing communications that affirm the desire to be united.

Navigating Mixed Feelings
When Deciding to Separate

People who are considering separating from their partner often experience a lot of indecision. This uncertainty manifests itself in many ways. One day, they wake up thinking they want to end the relationship, and another day, they wake up afraid of making a mistake and want to continue in the relationship. Some people, faced with the same uncertainty, make an effort to have happy moments to tilt the balance towards staying in the relationship. This may depend on their personality, decision-making style, degree of independence, and economic situation, as well as being influenced by social pressures.

Some factors, for example, are related to the personality of the decision-maker. If you are impulsive and do things without much thought, you will likely announce the breakup in an emotional moment. On the other hand, if you reflect a lot before deciding, the separation is likely to be prolonged. In these cases, the delay in making a decision is not due to a lack of information or possible mistakes but to the habit of overthinking and postponing what can be decided or done. The decision will take time, not because you need more information or because you might be wrong, but because it is your habit to think and postpone what you could already decide or do.

People who tend to avoid taking risks also have a lot of difficulty separating. If they have never lived independently, the idea of separating may cause them a lot of anxiety because they do not have the experience of managing the tasks and responsibilities of a home without the help or companionship of another person who supports them. For example, there are people who have never slept alone in a room, which may be related to unresolved nighttime fears. As children, they shared a room with a sibling and then left the parental home after getting married. When separating, fear and anxiety can arise from being alone, not necessarily because of the end of the relationship. Among the questions I asked people considering separation, I always asked if they had overcome nighttime fears. I worked with many people, men, and women, to overcome these nighttime fears, and, as a result of that, the distress associated with separation disappeared.

Also, it will be difficult for you to make the decision to separate if you are a person who tends to stay firm with the commitments you've made, even if they do not suit you or are not healthy. Some people have been educated since childhood on the value of keeping their promises and facing the negative consequences that might bring on. The mere thought of breaking a promise and letting others down causes them a lot of discomfort and shame. If you are that type of person, you are likely to see separation as a weakness of character and a failure, especially if there was a wedding and public event to celebrate the union and love. However, to err is human; many times, when we make commitments we do not have the experience or strength to adequately and wisely evaluate those decisions or to carry them out. Some neuroscientists claim that our brains often cannot anticipate the future or fully understand "lifetime" commitments. At the moment, it may seem right, but over time and experience, we discover that it is no longer so. When I asked large groups of married women if they would marry again knowing what they know now, many of them responded no. Even women with many years of marriage and children have shared that when they fell in love, they did not give themselves enough time to get to know their partners before accepting the marriage proposal. They felt ambivalent and had reservations but did not dare to end the commitment. In the present, they may repeat the pattern that led them to make mistakes in the past, but they can choose to do it differently. If you wish but find it difficult due to your nature, you can seek the help of a professional in human behavior. However, it's important to remember that the decision ultimately lies with you, and self-reflection is crucial in this process.

On the other hand, no romantic relationship is perfect or ideal because they are not free of conflicts. In the interaction with another human being, especially in an intimate relationship, there are always areas of difficulty and possibilities for improvement. It is not appropriate, then, to decide to separate simply because of conflicts and difficulties. You must evaluate the positive aspects of your relationship and put them on a scale alongside the negatives. Let's see the example of

Lourdes, who, after 10 years of marriage, decided to separate. Her list was as follows:

Positives	Negatives
Hardworking	He doesn't listen to me (there have been no changes)
Intelligent	He doesn't' take care of me (he has changed very little)
Athletic	If I get sick, he doesn't help me (there is no change)
Good friend	He always wants to impose himself (there is no change)
Helpful to others	He doesn't understand me when we argue (there is no change)
Handsome	Irresponsible

Of all the unfavorable circumstances in the list, the most intolerable for Lourdes was his irresponsibility. From the beginning of the relationship, she worked to ensure the payment of bills, in addition to having to remind her husband of appointments, commitments, and important details. Despite her many attempts to improve the relationship, she never observed a significant change in him. Lourdes made the decision to separate after realizing that her partner's irresponsibility put her in a role more akin to a mother than a wife.

On the other hand, do not consider the absence of negative aspects as something positive. Because someone is not an alcoholic, is not verbally aggressive, does not impose his whims is something in their favor but it does compensate for the absence of other positives. The lack of communication, emotional distance, financial irresponsibility, and lack of support can also be detrimental to a relationship.

For instance, after 15 years of marriage, Vivian considers the idea of separating from her husband. She describes him as "very good because he doesn't drink, doesn't smoke, doesn't abuse me, and isn't unfaithful." When asked if he positively influences her life, she can only say that he doesn't cause her problems. However, Vivian wants to separate because her husband is also not affectionate, doesn't converse with her, the sex life is practically non-existent, and he does not contribute financially to the household.

If your partner does not mistreat you, you should not consider this a positive element since it is not supposed to happen. It is simply the absence of something negative. When evaluating your partner's negative characteristics, ask yourself since when they have existed and if there has been a significant change in the last few months. If your partner is dishonest but a year ago lied more than now, for example, perhaps you can identify a pattern of improvement. If so, take that progress into consideration when evaluating the relationship. If even so, the final result is that there are more negative than positive aspects, and if you add that changing one of those negative aspects takes a long time and your partner does not show a willingness to make the effort to change, you can seriously consider separation as an option.

Before making a decision, it is important to consider seeking professional help or counseling. This can provide a neutral space to address relationship issues and work toward a resolution. It is important, however, that when deciding you take into consideration how long it will take to resolve the conflicts. Personality traits and patterns, for example, cannot be easily changed. They require the person to recognize the need for change and be motivated to achieve transformation. They also need a continuous, firm, and significant effort because merely wishing for change is not enough. Among the personality traits that can be problematic in a relationship are dependence (not being self-reliant or taking the initiative), authoritarianism, irresponsibility, difficulty committing, vices, difficulty expressing oneself, introversion, rigidity, stubbornness, dishonesty, difficulty respecting others, dishonesty, chauvinism, difficulty controlling aggressive impulses, selfishness, egocentrism, narcissism, sadism, and negligence.

On the other hand, it is important to understand that situations such as emotional and physical abuse are so detrimental to the well-being and mental health of both individuals that typically, when present in a relationship, separation is often the wisest option. We will be addressing emotional and physical abuse in more detail later on. Infidelity, abandonment, disregard, and lack of respect in the relationship can only be changed when significant effort is made by both parties. Addictive behaviors, such as alcoholism, drug addiction, and gambling, also tend to take a long time to overcome.

Another criterion you should consider when deciding

whether to separate or continue is the degree of personal growth you have achieved within your relationship. Compare the life you had before joining your partner with the one you have now. Evaluate how the relationship has helped or hindered the quality of your relationships with others, your level of self-esteem, your good qualities, and your shortcomings. If the balance of this comparison leans towards personal growth and improvement, the discomfort you feel in your relationship may be temporary. If, on the contrary, the balance leans towards continuous, albeit slow, deterioration, you should consider the need for significant change, which could include the option of separation.

It is true that sometimes close individuals may have a more objective perspective on the relationship and may point out aspects that the couple themselves do not see. It is crucial to consider different viewpoints before making such an important decision as separation. People tend to see more clearly social isolation, abandonment of goals, and personal neglect. Ask the people close to you how they see you so that you can make a better assessment of the impact of your relationship on you and your partner. For example, ask yourself, "Has my partner progressed and grown while I have remained stagnant?"

Numerous individuals do not realize how personality traits can affect their romantic relationship until they are deeply involved. It is important to be aware of these potential issues and address them constructively. These characteristics must be recognized and evaluated to determine how they affect the relationship before making consequential decisions. On the other hand, it is crucial to understand that although situations have the potential to improve, one must consider how long the process of improvement will take and how slow or fast progress will be. It is up to each person to decide whether they are willing to try to resolve relationship conflicts regardless of how long it takes. The romantic relationship is unique and personal; only you know your limits and how far you are willing to go.

It is a common belief that, given more time, a failing relationship could be saved. Time can help heal some painful experiences but time is not a cure or solution for character traits or bad habits. If you understand that your relationship has had an overall pattern of deterioration, you need to make a change. Many people have asked me if their relationship has a chance, even if their partner refuses to participate in resolving conflicts. It is essential to understand that if your partner does not participate, significant conflicts will not be resolved even if you give many more opportunities. Separation could be a healthy option if you have tried to improve the relationship and sought help, but your partner has not participated in those efforts.

Although every relationship requires hard work, there are certain unions that should not continue. In those cases, the decision to separate is the wisest, albeit the most difficult. Even though you have reached the understanding that the romantic relationship is unhealthy, the process of initiating the breakup may be a very difficult one. It's important to remember that making this decision can also bring a sense of relief and a new beginning. Furthermore, understanding that a relationship must end does not mean you will be able to separate immediately because the breakup process is complex. Following thru on the decision to separate can be postponed due to economic factors, children, fear of loneliness, and fear of the reactions from the partner, close friends, and family members.

People who regret separating, upon reflecting on what they have learned after the separation, often blame themselves for having taken too long to make the decision and follow thru on it. Decisions always involve risks, as the future is uncertain.

There are no guarantees or crystal balls that can show you the future. Only by experiencing the separation will you know if it was a wise decision. You cannot predict the future, so deciding today based on an unknown tomorrow is impossible. You can make estimates and projections, and make the necessary efforts to be informed about your decisions, but it is generally not possible to achieve a high level of certainty that you are making the perfect decision. Only by experiencing the separation will you know if it was a wise decision. Do not expect yourself to act today as if you have the wisdom you will gain tomorrow.

The Fear of a Partner's
Violent Reaction

It's important to understand that falling in love with an abusive person often begins with a promise of happiness and love. The experience of those who suffer psychological or physical abuse in their relationship is that they fall in love with someone who initially does not seem dangerous to them. These relationships start like many others. Someone approaches them and then proceeds to convince them that they will be happy with them. In a combination of courtship strategies and promises of a life of love and prosperity, the partner becomes convinced they are with the person who will make them happy. The initial infatuation stage of courtship is rarely experienced with instances of aggressive or dangerous behavior. Typically, this behavior arises when the abuser, unconsciously or consciously understands that they already have control over their victim. They know what to say and do to make her forgive them or not realize that she is experiencing abuse.

There is a pattern of many manipulative behaviors that cloud the judgment of the victim. For example, when an incident of insults occurs, it is very likely to be accompanied by an explanation and accusation that she provoked him. He makes her responsible for triggering his anger and lack of control. Therefore, the only thing that needs to happen to prevent the behavior from repeating is for her not to provoke him. For instance, don't look at others, don't prepare my food that way, don't question me, etc. If she behaves, he will, too. If the behavior involves excessive control over her, it is because he believes he has the duty to protect the relationship, and she does not realize how her behavior is putting them in danger.

The pattern of emotional and physical abuse during the romantic relationship often manifests with periods and behaviors associated with love alternated with others of verbal and physical aggression. In a relationship where the life and emotional well-being of the partner are at risk, not every day is violent. This duality of experiences and other elements makes it very difficult for the victim to understand that the relationship is toxic and will not change.

For the abused person, several factors make her doubt her perception and decision to end the relationship. Ambivalence is compounded by the fear of worsening her situation or even losing her life by deciding to separate. Beyond understanding that she is not to blame, she must realize that love will not change her partner. His love for her or her love for him will not alter the situation. It is a very complex problem, and even with professional help, it takes a lot of time to change. Usually, before any significant change occurs several relapses and incidents that endanger the life and mental health of the partner and children happen.

Although relationships vary widely, some crucial elements of how violence and abuse occur can be identified. To begin with, not all abusive individuals are the same. Some people abuse emotionally and verbally without ever raising a hand to assault you. Their treatment of their partner destroys self-esteem, causes insecurities, isolates their partner from important people who could contribute to their well-being and leads to economic dependence. Over time, the victim loses trust in their family and friends, doubts their own judgment, and feels incapable of leading an independent life, living in constant fear.

If making the decision to end a relationship is difficult, it is even more challenging for victims of abuse. The ability to make decisions is one of the areas that most weakens in this type of relationship. Typically, they are not allowed to make decisions for themselves. This is where friends and family can play a crucial role. By providing a supportive and non-judgmental environment, they can help the victim regain their confidence and make the necessary decisions for their well-being.

I remember one of my clients, an executive woman, telling me how she realized that her relationship was unhealthy when she hesitated to choose a 35-cent can of beans at the supermarket, despite making significant decisions involving thousands of dollars at her job. She felt pressured to avoid making mistakes due to her partner's harsh reactions. In another example, a mature and intelligent man shared that he felt like he was walking on eggshells when he came home because of his wife's unpredictable and violent reactions. He did not even feel safe announcing his arrival for fear of her response.

On the other hand, the abuser fails to accept that abuse negates any positive aspects of the relationship. When their partner informs them that they will not continue in the relationship unless the abusive behavior changes, the abuser often cannot grasp the seriousness of the situation. Many initially believe that their partner will change their mind and stay. If there have been incidents of physical abuse, the abuser tends to hold their partner responsible for provoking their anger and aggression. They then apologize and promise not to hit or mistreat again.

However, over time, the abuse is repeated, along with periods of remorse and peace. In some cases, the emotional dependence of the abuser on their partner is so intense that instead of reducing the abuse they threaten or resort to more extreme forms of violence to ensure that the partner does not leave. Others resort to intimidation tactics and seek support from family members, friends, or religious leaders to intervene on their behalf. However, giving in to pleas and promises of change generally does not break the pattern of abuse. It is crucial to recognize that the problem lies with the abuser, not with their partner.

If you are someone who is abusive it is vital that you seek professional help. In cases of extreme emotional dependence and violent thoughts, you are in danger of not only provoking the death of your partner but also spending the rest of your life in jail or potentially committing suicide afterward, as history shows. Love is not enough to change the pattern of abuse. If you suspect that you are in an abusive relationship, it is essential to seek professional help and protection.

Some people avoid communicating their intention to separate for fear of their partner's reaction. They worry about being assaulted or that their partner may attempt self-harm. If your partner is aggressive and has little control over their impulses, you should seek professional help before announcing your decision to separate. Professional guidance is essential not only for the best way to communicate your intention but also for navigating the separation process itself. If your partner has previously threatened to commit suicide if the relationship ends, it is crucial to seek professional help before communicating your decision. Remember, it is not healthy to stay together out of fear of your partner's violent reaction because the relationship will end anyway. You are not helping your partner by remaining by their side out of fear or pity. Staying in the relationship for these reasons does not benefit your partner.

Trying to separate from an aggressive person can indeed pose a significant risk. Statistics on women murdered by their partners tend to show that they are more likely to be killed when they are in the process of separation than when they remain in the relationship. However, you also face a considerable risk by staying in the relationship. You should know that there are help centers for people who are abused by their partners. These centers are staffed by professionals experienced in intervening in abuse situations. They can guide you regarding your legal rights and available police protection options. While no professional can guarantee your safety, they can advise you on effective ways to protect yourself. Many women and men in abusive relationships have been helped by these centers and professionals and have been able to establish healthy and prosperous lives.

Caught Between a Rock and a Hard Place: Facing the Threat of Suicide

There are numerous people who threaten to take their own lives after a separation. Even the farewell letters left by suicidal individuals often blame their ex-partners for their actions. While it is true that a separation can cause great suffering, suicidal behavior is not inevitable. Suicide is the responsibility of the person who commits it, not their partner, no matter how much they may seem to be a victim. It is a wrong decision that the person makes in response to what they cannot change. Although many people consider suicide when separating from their partner, it is necessary to understand that separation does not cause suicide. If you are the one who decides to separate, your partner will likely be emotionally affected. Even if you have had conversations and have been clearly expressing   your dissatisfaction with the relationship, your decision may come as a surprise to your partner.

Hope, a powerful emotional strategy, often serves as a balm for the pain of accepting an unwanted reality. However, when hope is misplaced, it can hinder the acknowledgment of the need for change within the relationship. Hope can be a source of comfort in the face of a final breakup, as long as it the hope of overcoming the pain and moving forward. But when hope becomes a barrier to accepting the reality of separation, it can impede personal growth.

The person who refuses to accept that the relationship has ended looks for any sign that confirms their desires. If they hear words of encouragement like "Put it in God's hands," they tend to interpret it as a strategy that will make their partner regret and return instead of seeing it as an opportunity to find comfort despite the separation. Do not feed those illusions. You are not doing them a favor if you expect them to gradually realize that your decision is final. You must communicate in a simple, clear, and firm manner. Help professionals can guide you and help your partner find better alternatives to handle their distress over the separation. There are many other ways to overcome pain; it doesn't have to lead to death. Do not try to guide your suicidal partner yourself because they will not listen to you objectively and will misinterpret your actions. It is much more effective for an outsider, a neutral person to intervene in the situation. Help is also available for people with suicidal thoughts.

The Reaction of Family and Friends

The reaction of family and friends is a great concern for both the initiator of the separation and the one being imposed upon. For both members of the couple, their respective parents' opinions and acceptance of the decision are important. Some people wait, even until the death of their parents, to end a relationship out of fear of hurting their feelings or disappointing them. There are also those who separate from their partner but prefer not to tell their parents anything. Generally, couples tend to hide the difficulties in the relationship and present an image of harmony and unity so as not to cause concern to their family and friends.

Many individuals, out of a sense of pride, conceal their relationship problems, hoping to maintain the illusion of a successful union. However, this often leads to a heavy emotional burden, as most close friends and family members can sense the underlying conflicts. The more you shield your loved ones from the truth, the harder it becomes for them to comprehend and accept your decision to separate, as it contradicts the image of stability and strength you've projected of your relationship.

When telling your relatives and close friends about your decision to separate, it's important to communicate clearly and decisively. Even if they don't agree with your decision, being precise in your communication will help them understand where you stand. It's natural for them to feel angry or sad about the separation, but their feelings shouldn't pressure you into changing your mind. Some relatives' reactions to breakups are influenced by societal expectations. In many cultures, a successful and happy family is defined by the number of married children and grandchildren. When breakups happen, they may take it as a reflection of their own image and feel like they've failed in their role as parents. It may be hard for them to accept that relationships don't always last. Give them time to adjust and try to disregard others' opinions. If your family and friends value social status more than your happiness, you shouldn't be overly concerned with their distress.

In reality, the suffering for everyone, including you and your partner, would be much greater if you remain in a relationship that is not healthy or does not satisfy you.

On the other hand, when family and friends understand that a person is resolute about their decision to separate, they tend to share information about their partner that they had kept secret to avoid causing problems. It is not uncommon for, acquaintances to reveal details about possible infidelities, conflicts, or faults of the partner after the decision to separate is announced. Many people truly get to know who their partner is only after announcing the separation; at that moment, they discover a reality that others had hidden from them. Sometimes it turns out that many knew what the spouse was doing except their partner.

When it comes to the decision to separate, it's crucial that you take the lead in communicating this to your family and friends. If your partner makes the announcement, they may deliberately or inadvertently shift the narrative in their favor, leaving you to be perceived as the aggressor. This is a common pitfall, as the initiator of the separation is often seen as the wrongdoer. However, the situation can escalate if your partner is the one that announces the separation. Do not delegate such an important communication to your partner. It's important not to succumb to the temptation to make the situation easier for your partner or to fear directly facing people close and important to you. By taking control of this important yet difficult communication, you can ensure that your perspective is heard and understood.

Separation is very difficult for people who maintain family and friendship relationships solely through their partner. Upon separation, these people will be without the support of friends and family. This often happens to those who cut ties with their family of origin and friends and only socialize with their partner's close circle. At the moment of separation, these people are left without a support network. Generally, during breakups, families tend to support their natural children, and friends tend to support the person who initiated the friendship. If you are considering separation, you must re-establish your own family and friendship relationships. It is a good time to rekindle those relationships you have abandoned or establish new friendships.

It's not uncommon for individuals going through a separation to seek the support of a third person. This could be a coworker, a friend, a counselor, a lawyer, or someone they are attracted to. This third person can serve as a neutral sounding board, helping to keep your needs in perspective. They can provide a safe space to vent and express your fears, anger, and sadness. They can also remind you of important facts, such as the fact that your partner had promised to change and never fulfilled their promise. This support can be crucial in helping you stay firm in your decision, even when your partner expresses that the separation makes them suffer and they need help.

The guiltier the person initiating the separation feels, the more tempted they will be to make the process easier for their partner. At that moment, a third person can help you have a fairer perspective for both parties. It is important to choose a trusted person to support you in the separation process. If you do not have that trusted person or find the breakup process very difficult, consider receiving help from a professional counselor, whether a social worker, lawyer, or psychologist. Remember, above all, they must be someone you consider competent, objective, willing and able to support you.

Communicating the Decision: Approaching the Topic of Separation with Empathy and Understanding

When someone decides to end a relationship, they often face difficulties in figuring out how to communicate this decision. They may fear that their partner will react with violence, emotional distress, or refusal to accept the decision. Keeping such a significant decision a secret can be very uncomfortable, especially if the relationship has been strained due to communication issues. As the desire to separate grows, individuals may begin to avoid their partner due to the anxiety and fear of having to openly discuss the decision. This might lead to reduced sharing and communication, as well as avoiding meaningful contact. Some individuals may find it challenging to maintain eye contact with their partner, fearing that their decision will become apparent.

Other people, sometimes without realizing it, seek to provoke the other person into verbalizing the idea of separating. Let's look at an example:

Angel noticed that his wife had avoided his presence. She didn't call him on the phone, went to bed before or after him, and didn't speak to him when they coincided at home. If he approached her, she withdrew. If he tried to kiss her, she moved away. Angel felt so uncomfortable with the situation that he confronted his wife: "Do you no longer love me? Do you no longer want to be with me?" The wife's behavior had finally caused Angel to express what she dared not communicate. However, bringing difficulties into the relationship rarely accomplishes the hidden goal of forcing the other person to make the decision for you and often results in a more deteriorated relationship. When they finally talk about separation it is in a much more difficult environment.

Another clear example of this is when unfaithful individuals leave love letters or items from their lovers in places where their partner can find them, leading to separation. Even if the other person initiates the separation process, it is the unfaithful person who has actually triggered the breakup. Some even make unreasonable requests. Here's a very common example I'd like to share:

Marta has noticed for some time that her husband comes home late from work and that on weekends, he is absent for hours, saying he has been running errands. One night, he announces that he wants to have "space." She does not understand that request since she is not one to demand his attention or be demanding. When she insists that he explain, he cannot clarify what that "space" means, except that she should not ask where he is going or when he will return. Later, she discovers that he has a relationship with a coworker.

Indirectly communicating the desire to separate can often lead to misunderstandings and the avoidance of the problem. It is not uncommon for a person who does not want to separate to discover and understand that their partner is being unfaithful, but they avoid confronting their partner for fear of triggering a breakup. Others may sense that something is amiss in the relationship, but they do not necessarily believe that a separation is imminent.

Some people adopt a more affectionate, attentive, and understanding attitude instead of confronting the person who wants to separate. Instead of requesting separation, they strive to save the relationship, complicating the situation for the person who wants to separate. Often, these attempts to save the relationship turn out to be mistaken because they do not address the real problems in the relationship.

An example of this is a person who believes they should look more attractive to improve the relationship, but their partner wants to separate because they consider them too superficial. Suppose the person who does not want to separate finally manages to accept and communicate that the relationship is in a crisis. At the same time, they will also express their conviction that they can save it. Many people agree to their partner's request for a second chance, even when they are convinced that it will not have positive results. Some people give that second chance, hoping their partner will realize the relationship cannot be saved. Although they seem to be giving an opportunity for the relationship to work , in reality they do nothing to save the relationship and sometimes do everything possible for the attempt to fail.

Another indirect strategy that people who want to separate use is to wait for their partner to make a mistake or a commit a serious offense and then use it to justify and announce their decision to end the relationship. The problem with this strategy is that the partner sometimes makes no mistakes or errors. Some people even discover that their partners display exemplary behavior during this period as if they know they are under observation. Another example is people who wait for their partner to fall in love with someone else and leave. They pray for God to help them find someone new. Some take on the role of a matchmaker arranging "spontaneous" encounters.

Indirect ways of communicating the intention to end a relationship are often ineffective. Generally, the person who wants to separate ends up having to be very clear and specific. When they finally verbalize their definitive intention to separate, their partner reproaches them for not being honest from the beginning. It is crucial to understand that you only need to verbalize one phrase: "I want to separate from you.", " I want to end our relationship". The rest of the information you need to communicate will be in response to questions or accusations. Once you manage to verbalize the initial sentence, you just need to stand firm and not retract. Remember, the longer you wait to communicate your intention to separate, the more difficult it will be for you to express that first sentence. Additionally, you must consider that expressing your decision will never be more difficult than staying in a relationship you do not want. I assure you that if you choose an indirect way to communicate it, you will have many more complications in the long run.

Although the person who wants to separate may want their partner to understand that the relationship is no longer healthy, providing multiple clarifications often creates more confusion. It is common for people who do not want the separation or are not ready to for it to feel distressed when hearing their partner's decision. They find it very difficult to "understand" the reasons when, in reality, what they struggle with is accepting the reality of the separation. They also tend to become irrational and interpret any gesture of affection as a sign that the relationship could be saved.

If your partner tends to react emotionally to situations, it is normal for them to find it difficult to understand your decision to separate. Be brief in your statements, and do not try to convince them with countless examples. Leave the explanations for after the initial crisis when your partner is calmer. It is also necessary not to be ambiguous in your statements or send contradictory messages to make the situation less painful and easier for your partner. It does not mean you should be cruel and insensitive to your partner but rather be clear and firm in your decision.

Likewise, you must be consistent in your actions. If you have communicated your intention to separate, do not continue to seek or call your partner. Although you may only want to make sure they are okay, your partner may misinterpret it as a sign that you want to maintain the relationship. Physical distance, although initially painful, makes it easier for both members of the couple to rebuild their lives. You need to understand that every time your partner sees or hears you, they will experience momentary relief, followed quickly by the pain of loss. If you miss your partner at certain times but remain determined in your decision, do not be selfish. Do not seek them out. Give them space to adjust to life without you.

Freeing Yourself from the Burden:
Guilt Feelings in Separation

The separation causes distress, so it is natural to perceive the situation as having a perpetrator and a victim. However, the person initiating the separation also experiences pain from the breakup and mourns the loss of their ideal of a stable relationship and the positive aspects of life as a couple. For many, this even implies the loss of their economic status, and their friends and family. On the other hand, the person who is on the receiving end of the separation is often unprepared for the breakup and suffers greatly, even if, they had previously considered the possibility of a break up. Sometimes the resistance to the separation stems from hurt pride, as it was their partner who initiated the split.

Likewise, the person initiating the separation often feels guilty for the pain their partner is experiencing and may consider themselves a bad person for seeking their own happiness. This guilt can lead them to give up their rights and accept unfair situations to make the separation process less painful for their partner. For example, they may take responsibility for shared debts, leave behind their belongings, and agree to unfair legal arrangements. On the other hand, the person on the receiving end of the separation may feel entitled to demand help from their partner. Let's see an example:

Nayda decided to separate after several failed attempts to save the relationship. When she communicated her decision to her partner, she felt extremely guilty. When her partner expressed financial concerns, so Nayda offered to assume all the debts. Additionally , her partner stopped contributing financially to the household, as Nayda would be the one staying in the apartment. However, her partner made little effort to find a new place to live, arguing that the apartments they visited were either too expensive or too far from work. Although Nayda considered the situation very unfair, she did not speak up about it, feeling responsible as she was the one who initiated the separation. This is just one example of how guilt can lead to accepting unfair situations in a separation.

It is crucial to understand that, to assume all the blame for the separation, you must have had all the responsibility. However, in a relationship, responsibility is shared. Both individuals contribute to the success or failure of the relationship. It's not fair to assume all the blame for the separation, as it takes two to tango. Often the person who feels guiltier is the one who has shouldered more responsibility throughout the relationship. This guilt can also haunt those who entered a relationship without loving their partner enough. They may have chosen the wrong person but didn't have the courage to admit it, believing their partner loved them too much. Others may confuse love with attraction and struggle to rectify that mistake.

Understanding that a relationship is neither a punishment, nor a sentence is essential. If someone makes a mistake in choosing their partner, they forfeit their right to happiness. Similarly, their partner deserves to be in a relationship where they are genuinely loved. Correcting the mistake as soon as possible is crucial so that both parties can rebuild their lives and find their happiness. If you realize that you do not love your partner, show courage and express your feelings as soon as possible.

The feeling of guilt can also arise when the person who does not want to separate requests a new opportunity and is denied. Generally, people tend to grant numerous opportunities, sometimes more than necessary. However, the opportunity not granted causes distress because it is thought that it could have been the one to bring about a change. If you have given many chances without seeing positive results, it is very likely that a new opportunity will not transform your partner. Although people seem motivated to change when faced with a request for separation, this motivation often diminishes once the breakup is postponed.

You should not feel guilty for not granting an additional opportunity, as it is not necessary, for example, to endure ten incidents of aggression or five of infidelity to decide to separate. When you understand that your partner has not changed or that you can no longer tolerate their behavior, that is the right time to act. Remember that your partner must respect your right not to be subjected to a situation of infidelity. Upholding your self-respect is key to making fair decisions.

The cycle of granting chances can create a false sense of hope and prolong the inevitable, making the separation even more painful for both parties. It's important to recognize that change must come from within and cannot be forced or expected simply because of the threat of a breakup. True, lasting change requires genuine commitment and effort, which often isn't sustainable if it's only driven by the fear of losing the relationship.

In these situations, it's crucial to prioritize your own well-being and mental health. While it's natural to feel guilty or responsible, remember that staying in an unfulfilling or unhealthy relationship benefits neither you nor your partner. By ending the relationship, you are giving both of you the opportunity to find happiness and fulfillment elsewhere.

The Fear of Loneliness
after Separation

When embarking on a romantic relationship, individuals are in search of a partner to share both the joyful and the sorrowful moments in life. They long for companionship for social activities, whether out in public places or at home. In a cohabiting relationship, there is also the beautiful opportunity to share tasks, belongings, and friendships. While most wish for companionship, the harsh reality is that many couples are faced with the heart-wrenching decision to part ways. In many cases, the decision to separate means starting a new chapter alone, which often leads many individuals to settling for unsatisfying relationships.

Loneliness is indeed one of the most intense and

challenging emotions to navigate, and it can be felt even when surrounded by others. Many people describe it as a profound emptiness, a void that seems impossible to fill. This feeling seems to be accompanied by anxiety, restlessness, and a tendency to. underestimate oneself. The fear of loneliness often plays a significant role in the decision to stay in a relationship, even when it may no longer be fulfilling or healthy.

For some, the presence of a partner serves as a buffer against the emptiness they fear. The idea of having someone to share a bed with or simply to be around at home can provide a sense of comfort and security. However, this can lead to postponing a necessary separation, as the thought of facing loneliness can be overwhelming.

It is important to recognize that while the fear of loneliness is valid, staying in an unfulfilling relationship can also lead to a different kind of loneliness-one where you feel isolated despite being with someone. Building a fulfilling life on your own, where you find joy and contentment in your own company, can be a powerful antidote to this fear. Engaging in activities you love, connecting with friends and family, and seeking professional support if needed can help you navigate this challenging transition and ultimately lead to a more fulfilling and independent life and a better future relationship with a new partner.

There are indeed people who, when faced with solitude, experience intense fear by imagining scenarios such as the presence of spirits, assaults, or natural disasters. This fear can be so overwhelming that they avoid being alone at all costs, which unfortunately which unfortunately prevents them from discovering that these fears are often transient and surmountable. It is completely natural for the first few days after a separation to be particularly challenging. During this period, h fear and anxiety can be heightened, and it may feel as though your world is falling apart. If you are someone who seek company out of a fear of loneliness, you might never overcome that fear unless you confront it head-on. There are several strategies you can employ to manage and eventually overcome this fear. For instance , turning on the television, lights, or radio can create a sense of presence and reduce feelings of isolation. Engaging in activities like reading, praying, or even rearranging the furniture in your home can also be very effective. These activities not only keep you busy but also help to distract you mind from fearful thoughts. By keeping yourself occupied and gradually getting accustomed to being alone, you may find that your fears are unfounded. Over time, you might even come to enjoy solitude, finding it a time for self-reflection, relaxation, and personal growth. You may find that you can enjoy solitude. You will learn to be your own company, to enjoy the time you spend alone, and to value the people with whom you share your space and time with. Try to surround yourself with people who enrich you and make you feel good. The key is to take small steps and be patient with yourself as you navigate this transition.

If you are considering separation, start by taking on tasks that will help you become more independent. This can be a gradual process that allows you to envision and prepare for a life without your partner. For example, begin by doing the shopping for items your partner typically buys, this will help you get accustomed to managing your own needs and preferences. Try cooking meals for yourself. This not only helps you become more self-sufficient but also allows you to explore and enjoy your own culinary tastes. Pay the bills or at least create a budget that does not rely on your partner's financial contributions. Understanding your financial situation is crucial for your independence. Identify the household tasks your partner usually handles and practice doing them yourself. This could include anything from laundry to home maintenance.

Keep in mind that at first, you may feel anxiety and discomfort. These feelings are natural and part of the process. As you continue to take on these tasks, you will likely start to feel more confident and capable. Consider reaching out to friends, family, or a therapist for support during this transition. Having a support system can provide emotional stability and practical advice. By taking these steps, you will gradually build a sense of independence and security. This preparation can make the process of separation less daunting and help you feel more in control of your life. Remember, the goal is to empower yourself and ensure that you are capable of managing your own needs and responsibilities.

The Separation and its Impact on Children

The process of separation can be more challenging for those who have children. Many who wish to separate choose to stay in the relationship to protect their children from the negative impacts of divorce. However, it is crucial to remember that children should not be the foundation of a romantic relationship, nor should child custody or divorce terms be disputed out of selfishness or the desire to cause pain to the ex-partner.

It is essential to understand that many children are emotionally scarred by the conflictive relationship between their parents. A separation or divorce may be a significant and difficult change that leads to growth and a healthier home environment. It can, however, be traumatic for the children if not handled adequately. It is unwise to involve children in the decision-making process, promote division's or ask them to take sides. They deeply resent the abuse, fights, and distance they witness and perceive. Even if your children are intelligent and appear mature enough to handle the emotional situation, they are not ready to be directly exposed to the grown-up process of separation. Furthermore, children tend to mimic their parents' behaviors and may act similarly as adults. For example, many mistreat their partners and children in the same way experienced with their own parents. Carefully evaluate what your children are learning from your romantic relationship and decide if that is what you want for their future.

During separation, it is important to communicate to your children how the breakup will affect their daily lives directly. You should explain to them which aspects of their lives will change and which will remain the same. If necessary, inform them if they will have to change schools, move to a new house, which parent they will live with, and when they will see each other. Providing specific information will help them make the necessary adjustments. Additionally, it is vital for parents who decide to separate to show mutual respect and avoid mutual accusations or attempts to paint their ex-partner as the villain in front of the children. It is important to remember that the relationship that is ending is that of the couple, not that of the parent and child.

Establishing a new but stable routine with your children is important, it's reassuring. This stability will give your children a sense of security and confidence during this challenging time. Changes are more easily tolerated when maintained in an environment of stability and trust. Keep in mind that remaining in a home environment where there is frequent conflict and tension between the parents has a negative impact that is multiplied by the time it is prolonged. The least amount of time of being exposed to this toxic environment the better for all concerned.

Establishing a new but stable routine with your children is important and reassuring. This stability will give your children a sense of security and confidence during this challenging time. Changes are more easily tolerated when they occur in an environment of stability, trust and love. Keep in mind that remaining in a home environment where there is frequent conflict and tension between parents has a negative impact that is exacerbated the longer it continues. The less time spent in this toxic environment, the better for all concerned. If you find that you need support and help in managing these challenges seek professional help. Speaking to a professional will not only help you better understand your role and explore your options, but it also provides a safe space to ventilate your emotions and frustrations without the fear of negatively affecting those who are exposed to listening to the intimate details.

It is crucial to provide a stable and loving environment for your children, even during times of personal upheaval. Open communication, reassurance, and maintaining routines can help mitigate the negative impact of a separation. Seeking professional guidance, such as family therapy, can also be beneficial in navigating this challenging transition and ensuring that the emotional well-being of your children is prioritized.

The Separation Process:
Steps and Considerations

Although there are various ways to end a relationship, all entail a certain degree of emotional pain. Those who decide to separate often seek a way to minimize suffering for themselves and their partner. Sometimes, a gradual separation is attempted, with the hope that the pain of the breakup will be less intense if it is done slowly. However, this type of separation can generate more distress, as the constant presence of the person initiating the separation can feed the hopes of the other party. The more contact you maintain with your partner, the more likely you are to convey your indecision about the separation. This will make adapting to the change and rebuilding your individual lives difficult. Gradual separation is a strategy that often creates more problems than it solves.

Do not prolong the process of physical separation from your partner. Although achieving an abrupt separation is difficult and uncommon, you should also not prolong the breakup process. Preparing for the separation and making the necessary economic adjustments is crucial. If you are considering separation, avoid participating in joint purchases of a house, a car, or valuable items that represent a significant and long-term commitment to your partner.

The division of shared assets can also be a challenging and emotionally charged process. Some people may avoid making the corresponding divisions to avoid conflicts. Although giving up all belongings to the partner may seem like the easiest and less conflictive option at the time, many regret this decision once the initial impact of the separation has passed. Assets such as the house, furniture, clothes, cars, pets, and savings represent the lifestyle that was shared as a couple. Therefore, it may be tempting to relinquish these to eliminate any reminders of the relationship. However, if this is your case, it would be more beneficial to take what belongs to you and then decide whether you want to sell or give it away. Do not give up your belongings on impulse, as you may regret it later, especially if your ex-partner seems to be living comfortably while you are not. It is helpful for both of you to make a list of your respective belongings and only negotiate those items that appear on both lists. It is not necessary to discuss every item on the list. If significant conflicts arise, seeking the assistance of a lawyer or impartial friend can be reassuring and beneficial. They can provide guidance and support during this challenging process.

The laws that establish the requirements for a legal divorce and the rights of each party indeed vary depending on your location. These laws are typically outlined in public documents, such as state or country-specific family law statutes, which you can access through government websites or local legal libraries. It's crucial to take the time to read and understand all the details involved in the divorce process. If you find any part of the legal language confusing or overwhelming, seeking orientation and legal advice from a qualified attorney or legal aid service is highly recommended. They can help clarify your rights and obligations, ensuring that you are well-informed and prepared for the legal proceedings ahead.

Frequent phone calls after the separation can prolong the adjustment period to the breakup. It is common for the person initiating the separation to receive calls from their ex-partner, in which they may complain, threaten, or simply seek an excuse to keep the relationship alive, even if only over the phone. Although you should not be cruel, it is important to be firm in avoiding this type of communication. If your ex-partner does not understand or respect the boundaries you set, then it may be necessary to take more drastic measures, such as changing your phone number or requesting that their calls not be put through to you. Call and text blockers on cell phones can be helpful in these cases, as they allow you to select which calls you want to respond to.

It is crucial to avoid calling your ex-partner when you feel bad, as this could potentially cause them emotional distress and complicate the healing process for both of you. It is common for the person initiating the separation to seek comfort from their ex-partner during difficult times. Some people even insist on maintaining a friendship with their ex-partner without understanding how painful it can be for the other person. Recognize the pain your ex-partner may be experiencing, and do not demand that they be your friend at this time. You may achieve this once they have adapted to the separation.

Instead, reach out to a trusted friend or family member to share your feelings and seek support. Friends can provide a listening ear, offer advice, and help you navigate through your emotions in a healthier way. Additionally, consider engaging in activities that bring you comfort and joy, such as exercising, pursuing hobbies, or even seeking professional counseling if needed. This approach can help you build a support system and develop coping mechanisms that do not rely on your ex-partner.

Handling the Perception
of Abandonment

When the partner announces the desire and intention to separate it is a profound emotional experience. For many it is as emotionally challenging as the death of their partner. It's important to remember that going through a separation is a normal part of life, and experiencing the typical stages of grief is a natural response to losing a loved one. Initially it's common to deny the reality of the situation and feel stunned when your partner expresses a desire to end the relationship. You might find yourself preferring to believe that your partner simply needs time to reflect. Even as you begin to accept the separation, you may still try to hold onto the illusion that the relationship is permanent. If your partner has expressed their intention to separate, it's normal to feel surprised or in crisis.

However, the longer you take to move past this initial phase, the harder it will be for you to adapt to reality. It's crucial not to insist on ignoring reality, as this will only prolong the process.

Once people accept the separation, they tend to idealize the ex-partner and the relationship, intensifying the sense of loss and increasing the belief that they cannot live without their partner. However, nobody is perfect, so it is likely that your partner had their flaws. The more deficiencies of your partner you can identify, the less painful the process will be. Take stock of both the good and the bad aspects in the relationship; perhaps your close friends can help you with this.

Feelings of guilt and the desire to reverse the situation are common in the person to whom the separation has been imposed. This person often tries to understand what went wrong, mistakenly thinking that if they identify ithe cause, they can save the relationship. However, it is important to remember that relationships deteriorate for multiple reasons and is due to the responsibility of both parties. Even if you manage to identify some of your faults, your partner's faults still need to be acknowledged. If, after the separation, you decide to change or improve the flaws your partner identified in you, you must do it as a personal growth goal. This is necessary because if you manage to make the changes and your partner still does not return to the relationship, you will feel like you have made efforts in vain. It is important to do everything for yourself and not to save the relationship.

If you want to overcome the separation, you will have to fight against the unhappiness you will feel at the loss of your partner. It is common for feelings of discouragement, disorientation, irritability, and confusion to arise during a breakup. Many people experience episodes of crying that come without warning. Others feel an intense pain in the chest, and have difficulty breathing. Some people start to have trouble sleeping, neglect their physical appearance, and may see their professional and family performance affected. However, if you manage to make the necessary adjustments, you will find that these symptoms are temporary.

Establishing a daily routine and resisting the temptation to isolate yourself, to cry yourself to sleep is crucial. Even if you don't feel like it or have the energy, it is necessary to force yourself to leave the house, take care of your appearance, perform tasks, and socialize with people who can support you.

Although at first, you may not be able to maintain a high level of activity, over time, you will regain your energy.

If you are not in the mood for activities, it is advisable to gradually incorporate them. Do not push yourself too hard. If you are at work and feel sad or feel like crying, dedicate a brief time for yourself. For example, you can reserve five minutes of each hour to go to a save place and cry. Force yourself to wait until those five minutes arrive to release your emotions. You can use work as a distraction but do not suppress your feelings for eight consecutive hours.

It is also important to seek support from people who can listen to you and motivate healthy alternatives. You can also seek professional help to guide you through the process of overcoming the crisis. It is crucial to understand that anti-anxiety or anti-depressive medications without medical supervision, alcohol, and drugs are not effective solutions, even if they are suggested to you as temporary relief. Keep in mind that these substances can be addictive, potentially leading to an even bigger problem. Express yourself to the people who support you, but do so when they are available. If you talk to them while they are busy or interrupted, you will feel that they are not paying attention to you. It is better to have ten minutes of complete attention than five hours with constant interruptions.

Understanding that the end of a relationship is often a complex interplay of factors can help mitigate some of the pain. Seeking professional help, such as counseling, can provide a safe space to explore these emotions and develop coping strategies. Additionally, engaging in self-care activities and focusing on personal growth can help in moving forward and finding peace with the situation.

You must familiarize yourself with the skills necessary to lead an independent life. The goal is to build a life where you feel confident and self-sufficient. Research and seek guidance from your friends. This journey can be challenging, but it is also an opportunity for significant persona growth and self-discovery. If you manage to do this, you will feel better and turn the separation into a personal growth experience.

Final Reflections

Breaking the ties that bind two people is difficult and painful. However, that rupture is necessary when the relationship harms the growth and well-being of either person. This harm can manifest in various ways, such as emotional abuse, lack of support for personal goals, or a toxic environment. One should not insist on maintaining a relationship out of tradition or commitment if it genuinely does not serve the purpose of a romantic partnership.

People who come together out of love establish bonds that should promote the growth of each member of the couple. That's why, if attempts to salvage the relationship bear no fruit, it's necessary to focus on salvaging the individuals and break the bonds.

The process of separation is undertaken out of self-love and respect for the partner. The person to whom the separation is imposed, as well as the one initiating the breakup, needs to muster the courage to emerge successfully from the process. While it's painful and challenging, both individuals have the opportunity to develop a greater sense of individuality and self-worth. Don't fear the future just because you're experiencing difficult changes at this moment. Be brave and fight for your well-being.

Most people who decide to separate after careful consideration and responsible action tend not to regret their decision. For many, separation can represent liberation and a rediscovery of oneself. It's an opportunity for people to grow and learn to better appreciate what a romantic relationship entails.

I recommend not rushing into a new relationship after a breakup. Take time to get to know yourself again and reflect on the experiences you've been through. If you notice any patterns in yourself that need change, now is the time to work on them. If you feel overwhelmed, consider seeking professional help. It's essential to take this time to heal so that you can enter a new relationship with greater maturity and clarity.

www.ingramcontent.com/pod-product-compliance
Lightning Source LLC
Chambersburg PA
CBHW051545120626
46551CB00013B/1370